un(in)formed

un(in)formed

Becky Deans

BEARDED BADGER
PUBLISHING CO.

BEARDED BADGER
PUBLISHING CO.

Contents

Leicester

I made a list of all I'd lost to Leicester
My time, my way, a number of car parks
I tend to see this city as disaster
And many anxious days have left their marks
I freelanced in-house once but was sent packing
Tears ready to erupt as it was said
My branding understanding was lacking
The client would do the copy work instead
But still it gave me reason to explore
The inns and outs of this historic place
I found a king resting under the floor
Of a car park, now museum in its space
So though the client walked all over me
I got the chance to walk on royalty.

Codnor Common

It's hard to breathe now
Concrete covers and constricts
Carved-up urban lungs

Weighted

We walk with school bags weighted on our backs
Defined by cruel labels others chose
We stoop to follow predetermined tracks
Our arms outstretched to deal with fortune's blows
Our dreams defeated soon as they appear
Our sights revised in line with cuts or costs
We take the path that seems to us more clear
And dare not even think of what we've lost
And later, when we break out of our mould
And do the things we really want to do
Our inner voices say, "don't be so bold
You're scared to face the fear of something new"
Ignore the voice of doubt, don't let it win
No future's fixed, you can let life begin.

Mrs Thomas de Quincey

"Not quite the right sort"
 the report of the poet with a PhD
 in snobbery, the Lakeland straight man
 William Wordsworth.

"What are you thinking, giving a ring
to a milkmaid? Affairs are one thing
marriage something else," he said, pacing
around the room in elegant feet.

"I mean, just think where her hands
have been," he protested, dabbing his
troubled forehead with a finely starched
handkerchief, wringing it out

Onto the ice-sleek polished floor,
watching the sweat drip, flicking
a lock of hair gone astray back
to the left, then to the right again.

De Quincey paced the room around
with his eyes, surprised by the
reaction of his friend, so keen to
lend his voice to the meek and poor

to champion the cause
of the idiots and the mad, then
Thomas became glad, because what he had
what he had, raised mountains

stopped streams in their tracks
and made his blood run hotter
than the sky. He had his life
and would let the others write.

Pantry

Brick-red eggs stand in line
On grey crown cups.

Earthenware pots glare outwards.
Boxes nestle

Cardboard on cardboard.
Spoons lie icy.

Our faces distort
in the harsh light

fighting through the cracked glass.
Mist turns to dust.

There we learn our grains and wheat
mix our oats.

The smooth white liquid
rattles in our throats.

Force-feeding

For the suffragettes

Wrapped in layers of wool, but still so cold
Feeling fierce but really not that well
She reads out loud the bible to the mould
To try to block the screams outside her cell
But soon the door slams open, she's held still
The vomit-smelling doctor brings a tube
That's dirty, and a funnel with old food
They force her mouth wide open, though she bites
And struggles hard with each brutal attempt
Yet soon they have a gap within their sights
And India rubber makes its forced decent
But as she lies sick and shivering on the bed
They can't control the freedom in her head.

What Shall We Do with the Boys?

Send them to the lines
For King and Country
Plaster them in hope

Give them a song to sing
As their hands, blown off
By bones, shatter around them,
Narrate their own story.

Lend them a girl to melt for
Blooming bosoms like two ripe canons
Then take them to a brothel
And give them the clap.

Send them a catalogue
To feed their weary eyes
A tongue to pretend, perhaps,
That the biscuits, rotting their teeth

Could be roast beef and potatoes
Send them roast beef and potato
Imaginations to keep them.

Send them a Bible to bind them
Lend them a new suit to marry them
Then send out a stretcher to carry them.

Pastures New

There's nothing better than a new front door
Opening onto a new family life
The sharpness of a freshly tiled floor
The space for wedding photos: man and wife
A garden with a perfect square of grass
No shade of trees: small bushes yet to bloom
A gravel drive that crunches as you pass
A bathroom just about for every room
But still I miss the dirtiness of farms
Of cows, churning up this field as they run
The cockerel crows instead of alarms
And fields of corn cavorting in the sun
How will we put food on all of our plates
If living farms are turned to dead estates?

Dance

And the disco dancers go fast
Beating the air with their fists
Swinging their lips to the tune
of a cheat with a synth and a past.

They glitter and gleam in the glare
of lazers and cartoon characters
smashing display behind the DJ
as eyes spiral doves and delay.

And the disco dancers approach
the bloke with the burns and the roach
perched in the chill out blue zone
selling pills to pool out his thrill

from prancing feet and block heels
pounding the floor with the hype
of the man on the mic and the club friends
and life and the hugs and the mugs.

And the disco dancers go home
shivering from speed and from cold.
A teeter, a tikka, a night bus
a beaker of Horlicks, then sleep and then work.

When Did You Stop Learning Baby?

When they told you off at school?
When they told you kids should mess?
When they told you that you're thick?
When they made you wear that dress?

When the lads forgot their work
Took up studying your chest?
When you worked out it's not cool?
When they made you wear that dress?

When you won a full-time post
At the trainee manager's desk
But they made you make the tea?
When they made you wear that dress?

When you drank yourself again
To a state of helplessness?
When your period was late?
When they made you wear that dress?

When you gave it up for love?
When your house was in a mess?
When he only hit you once?
When your baby wore a dress?

Domestic

I know you love me really; you just fight it
You're mean and moody but I'm glad you're mine
I should have made the tea the way you like it

If there was a flame, I'm not sure I'd relight it
Our wedding vows have somehow lost their shine
I know you love me really; you just fight it

It's hard to live in such a changing climate
One moment you're malignant then benign
I should have made the tea the way you like it

You're different out in public to in private
But the fact that you're still with me is a sign
That of course you love me really, you just fight it

It's like you're a touch paper and I light it
But you make an effort when you've crossed the line
I should have made the tea the way you like it

I'd leave you but I don't think I'd survive it
I almost like you when I'm on the wine
I know you love me really; you just fight it
I should have made the tea the way you like it.

He Loved One Thing
Apologies to Anna Akhmatova

The smell of onion and garlic
Cooking, leaking out
Of her skin, branding her clothes.
That promise of a meal, ready to turn
With repetitive force.
The comfort of nothingness
Of whole countries debased with
The same roughly chopped onions and garlic
Browning, burning
In that wedding present pan.

Shred

You are my life, my completeness
This love is my weakness.

You're the treasure in my chest
My heart can't rest.

You're my before and my after
The absence of laughter.

I'm held. You're my holder.
My future is stuck in your folder.

My strength is this:
To shred the paper without looking,
To walk into the silence.

Slab

Put down a concrete slab, put down another
Put down concrete slabs everywhere, until
Concrete pervades everything, you, me
We're dusty and stuck, white-faced
Unable to move because we're part of the development
And your slab is our tomb.

Create new roads, bypass those roads
Then build a bypass bypass
So every place is connected and
No one ever has to stop to a chug in their cars
And all you can see for miles around at night is streetlights
Dazzling every single inch of the planet
So there is no night.

Throw up some houses, make it an estate
There's a square of ground there on those tarpits,
Throw up some more
It doesn't matter how small they are as long as
They have a patch of grass at the back and a hair's width
Between then. Pile them high, house upon
House upon house. Smother the earth with brick
And plaster and gravel. Build a tower of houses
So high you can see them from the moon.

Chop down the trees. They're in your way.
They litter the place with their leaves and seeds.
We don't need their drainage. We want empty
landscapes, nowhere to shelter, nowhere to run.
Nature's overrated. The planet is better
When we get together and sweep it all away.

Recipe for Success

There is no recipe for success
Just things that make you laugh or make you smile
Life is about the joy and nothing less

You might think that your life is just a mess
A mix of mouse droppings and bile
But there is no recipe for success

Take some potato peelings and press
Them into a dish, oven for a while
You'll get crisps - and joy - and nothing less

If you want to travel, do not stress
A Persian rug might move you for a mile
There is no recipe for success

Go shopping, get some new shoes and a dress
Parade around the streets or down the aisle
Life is about the joy and nothing less

If you're low in iron, eat watercress
For sweetness add some Tate and Lyle
But there is no recipe for success
Life is about the joy and nothing less.

Repossesion

It feels like we're being taught a lesson
By mother Earth, slow down, take stock
And brace yourself for the Great Depression

You might make mindfulness your mission
Keep busy, or lose it all in shock
Buy wine and start a drinking session

When memories come to haunt you, question
Their motives; know past is past; don't rock
And embrace the wave of great depression

As heroes walk among us, listen
To echoes of applause around the block
A great start to your drinking session

Don't give up; make a repossession
Of yourself; let opportunity knock
Choose projects over great depression

Make up your harmonic progression
Don't play your life in minor, or in schlock
Don't brace yourself for the Great Depression
Buy wine and start a drinking session.

Rosie

Can I catch your smile
Highlighting the happiness
Like giggling glitter?
I feed you up, make you strong
So you can totter away

Flute

Blow sideways, announce
(Change rhythm and tone)
The dead elephant rises
The puppet gestures
To beats of beautiful bone
The fertility of life

ACKNOWLEDGEMENTS

Thank yous: my husband and family; Emma Pass; Dwane Reads; everyone at Word Wise, Speech Therapy, Derby Performance Poetry and in the Derby and Nottingham poetry scene and beyond, Sophie Sparham, Leanne Moden, Trevor Wright, Emma Ireland, Daron Carey, DrayZera; the She Speaks collective; Furthest from the Sea.

Helen Mort and LoveLit Derbyshire for the poetry surgery as well as Derbyshire County Council and the Arts Council for Writing Ambitions funding.

For inspiration and workshops Jamie Thrasivoulou and Derby Museums (Flute); Charlotte Lunn and Scarthin Books (Codnor Common and Rosie); Tanvir Akram and Radio Derby (Reposession); George Szirtes and Writing East Midlands (Leicester); Bill Herbert and the Wordsworth Trust (Mrs Thomas de Quincey and Pantry); Derby International Women's Day team, past and present (Force-feeding); Ripley Writers' Group, particularly Alice Athena Hyde, Mary Hastings, Trish Kerrison, Robin Richards, Nick Snow, Bruce Brislin (Pastures New, Domestic, Recipe for Success, He Loved One Thing). David Brock for publishing 'Codnor Common' in 'The Lawrentian - Magazine of the Lawrence Players'.

Some of these poems have appeared on my Instagram (@writebeckydeans6) Facebook page (@writebeckydeans) and Wordpress blog (beckydeans.com).

TRA[verse]

For more information about the range of poetry on the TRA[verse] imprint, please visit:

www.beardedbadgerpublishing.com

or follow us on social media:

Facebook - **Bearded Badger Publishing**

Twitter - **@beardedbadgerpc**

Instagram - **@bearded_badger_publishing**